Therapy on Platform 9¾

Journeys through
Dissociative Identity Disorder

Patricia Hamilton

Therapy on Platform 9¾: Journeys through Dissociative Identity Disorder
Second edition, published in 2022 by Mono Unlimited

Please direct all enquiries to:
Patricia Hamilton
patricia.hamilt@optusnet.com.au
Copyright © Patricia Hamilton 2022

Editing:
First edition, edited by Diana Scott (Registered Psychologist, Music and Imagery Therapist)
Second edition, edited by Monique Lisbon (Mono Unlimited: Computer & Printing Support)

Book layout and cover design:
Monique Lisbon (Mono Unlimited: Computer & Printing Support, www.monounlimited.com)

Photo credits:
Cover photo and photo of author: Anna M. McKendry (Registered Nurse)
Photos of Dee's drawings: Amy J. Lacey (Artist, Art Therapist)

ISBN: 978-0-6453754-3-5 (paperback)

A catalogue record for this book is available from the National Library of Australia

DEDICATION

I dedicate this book to my father
Henry Joseph Buckman
who introduced me to classical music
and who taught me how to sit still and concentrate

CONTENTS

INTRODUCTION

When I open a book and look at the introduction I am often tempted to close it and never look at it again. When I do struggle through the introductory text I often get the impression that the whole story has been told so I don't have to read any further.

Relax – in writing an introduction, I promise I won't go into the guts of the stories! I only want to explain the title and why I have honoured JK Rowling (1997) by using her phrase, *Platform 9¾*. I found some striking similarities between Harry Potter and his search for the said platform, and my experience with many clients over the last thirty years or so. I also find the imagery useful in describing the process of embarking on a healing journey. You see, I believe that a healing journey has to start somewhere and go somewhere else. I can't take anyone anywhere until I meet them where they are: we both have to be on the same 'Platform' and sometimes the search for the right platform can be difficult.

In the first book of JK Rowling's *Harry Potter* series, named *The Philosopher's Stone* (1997), Harry is on his way to Hogwart's School of Wizardry. He has to first go to Platform 9¾ to catch the Hogwart's Express. Naturally, he cannot find the platform. He asks a porter who thinks he is just being smart. He hears a woman with several children, complaining about the overabundance of Muggles. Recognising this word for 'non-wizard folk', Harry follows them and meets up with the Weazleys. He asks if they know the way to Platform 9¾ and watches as the children, with their trolleys, head straight for the big brick pillar that stands between platforms 9 and 10. Just as they reach the wall and disaster appears imminent, the children disappear. Mrs Weazley advises Harry that if he is a bit scared, 'then it is best to get a bit of a run-up'. Harry follows her advice, and finds himself looking at the Hogwart's Express as it builds up a head of stream, ready for the journey.

I don't know how often, when working with a client, I have felt just like Harry. The energy is building, we could make a breakthrough, or we could end up in a bigger mess than when we started. I have to trust the process, to get a bit of a 'run-up', breathe into the feeling … and just keep going. This experience is quite common when I am working with Music and Imagery. The music has tapped into an issue and provided the imagery. The tension builds and all I can do is simply stay with the journey and trust the music, which comes in with what is needed at the time. The music may consist of stronger tones, or of softer, caring support that leads to a resolution.

In the chapters of this book, you will meet the very first person I recognised as dealing with dissociation and her alter-egos (aspects) who introduced themselves to me. This case taught me a lot about what to do – and, at the time, what not to do. I came out of that experience with a few rules about what I consider to be helpful and unhelpful. My views have changed over time and some of my 'rules' at the time have since been modified, because the basic premise I come back to is that I can't take a person anywhere unless I meet them where they are: forming a solid basis of trust which in turn allows alter-egos to reveal themselves to me and my client, who is often not even aware of their existence.

So as for now, it is time to 'take a bit of a run-up' and hopefully we can all witness the magic on Platform 9¾.

– Patricia Hamilton
Registered Psychologist
Music and Imagery Psychotherapist
NSW, Australia
November 2021

PART 1

Travelling with Dee

Stages of the Journey with Dee

As I reviewed my notes from this case, I discovered that the imagery of *Platform 9¾* was not the only thing that linked Harry with my client, Dee. As I grew to know her and she grew to trust me, I was called upon to enter into her world of magic – only she would not have called it 'magic' –and, at the time, neither would I. I would have preferred 'intuition' or 'extra-sensory perception' or even 'prophecy', not magic – and certainly not the kind that Harry encountered.

In the early days of therapy, Dee and I were both looking for the right platform. At times we were on one platform which looked promising for a while, and then we were on another. I sometimes had my sights set on a certain destination and I had to pull back from that. After all, there is not much point to me, the therapist, going somewhere alone. At other times, suddenly, without much warning, I would recognise that we were onto something important and we would go deeper into territory that we had not encountered before. All may go well for some time – then, without warning, the situation began to look more complicated once more, and I would once again wonder where we were heading. A brick wall seemed imminent, with a good chance of us ending up splattered against it! All I could hold onto was the knowledge that I must 'trust the process' and the belief that the answers were within both of us – and we must just keep going. This is what I did, trusting that we would end up in a magical place of healing and restoration.

Dee and I worked together over a period of almost two years; in that time I saw her for 60 sessions. She presented me with 105 drawings and 37 letters. I can recognise five main stages in my contact with Dee and the same themes arose in those stages – however, we seemed to meet them on a different level each time. The drawings and the letters in this book give a glimpse of what the process felt like from her point of view as we travelled along together.

Stage 1: April to September

Dee was in her fifties when I first met her in the early 1990s. She was referred to me by a Catholic priest. She wanted to talk about the death of her mother when she was nine years old, and the death of her husband, Keith, five years before our meeting. She also wanted to talk about the fact that she had been feeling 'very strange' and 'very odd' lately. She said that she had been having a lot of spiritual experiences, but she found it difficult to talk about these things because she was very embarrassed about them. At the time, I thought it best to put these on the back-burner. The grief work felt safer, as I had facilitated a lot of grief work and I wanted to get to know her before we launched into the spiritual realm. Also, if she was embarrassed by her 'spiritual' experiences it would be better to approach them with some degree of caution. I was also conscious of not wanting to transfer any of my particular beliefs onto her.

Grief

Dee had very clear memories of the day her mother was taken to hospital. She watched as she was carried out to the ambulance. It was a windy day and, as the wind blew the blanket off her mother, Dee thought, 'She will get a cold and die.' Dee never saw her mother again.

After her mother's death, Dee's father put her in the care of her aunt and left her. So Dee lost both parents that day. Her father hardly ever came to visit and she spent many years wondering what she did wrong to cause him to abandon her. She also said that she spent many years not believing that her mother was dead; always hoping she would return. During that time, she built up a picture of the 'ideal mother' who loved her more than anyone ever could.

When Dee was only 17, she married Keith and they subsequently had ten children. Raising ten children could not have been easy. When I asked her about the marriage, all she could offer was that it was 'very difficult', but the stubborn, distorted look on her face communicated more. After Keith's death, it seemed that Dee idealised him also to some extent, implying that her marriage was better than it was.

Over the course of therapy we worked with issues related to both of these deaths, alternating between the two. Dee acknowledged that some 'terrible feelings' were welling up inside her about both deaths. She was unable to identify what the feelings were or anything about them, so I encouraged her to draw anything that represent how she felt. She thought that was a silly idea but was prepared to try. To help her begin, I suggested she draw a house. Apparently she did draw a house, but I didn't get to see it for months because the drawings she brought in took up all her attention – especially Image 1 which she said 'frightened' her.

Image 1: Creature

We came to know the figure holding her in the drawing as 'Creature'. Creature often came with Dee to sessions, and also sat with her in the doctor's waiting room. The scary figure at the bottom appeared often in later drawings.

Talking about the drawings led her into deeper feelings around her mother's death, and reminded her of a recurring dream from childhood. In the dream she is running through a forest and all of the trees, which had serpents for branches, are reaching out to grab her. Later in the course of therapy, she drew this dream, and it became one of the significant points of healing for her.

The Church

Another theme which emerged at this time was Dee's association with the church.

This section could also be called 'Anger'. Dee said that she was angry with the church and all the man-made rules that made life so hard for ordinary people. One of her biggest fears was that she was also angry with God who, she believed, '... allowed bad things to happen to good people.' We had many discussions about this, and Dee shook her head in disbelief the day I said that God was the safest being to be angry with. No – her God was vengeful and punishing, and could strike you dead in an instant – in conflict with the loving Jesus who was a comfort to her.

The most frightening thing for Dee during this phase was that she was beginning to recognise how much anger she was holding. The anger was visible in her drawings and in her interactions with her family. There were many arguments with her children especially, which were very distressing for her.

Dee was a very caring person and, even while she was encountering difficult issues in therapy, she had other people drop in to spill their problems onto her. She recognised that they were draining her energy but she said they 'just couldn't turn them away.' She spoke of one person in particular, Gloria, as extremely draining, and pretty scary also. Gloria carried a couple of knives with her, just in case she felt the need to slice someone up for looking at her the 'wrong' way. It bears stating that Gloria was a real person who I also had dealings with. Hence, Dee's fear of her was not unrealistic.

Dee had good days and not-so-good days. She said that she was feeling a lot better and that she understood her drawings better. However, I certainly did not share her greater understanding of them. Whilst I had done some training in how to work with drawings (which was why I suggested she draw in the first place), these drawings left me totally puzzled. I remember sitting there looking at them, without a clue where to start. I did the usual thing and asked Dee about them, and she said that she didn't know either.

So we were both in the dark, staring at a series of puzzles. I had to accept that while her understanding of the drawings was becoming clearer to her, she was unable to explain them to me. I was pleased that she was beginning to understand them better even if I wasn't. The paradox that exists in the 'knowing', and not yet 'fully knowing', or not being able to verbalise it, showed up in many of the circumstances we were yet to encounter.

Additionally, Dee now declared that her path was a lot clearer to her and she knew what she had to do. She did not explain what form or direction that 'path' would take, but I knew that she would share it when she was ready. However while Dee may have felt that she was making some headway in understanding herself, the difficulties she experienced with some of her family continued to cause her ongoing distress.

Stage 2: September to December

The Accident

Three months into therapy, Dee was injured in a car accident; her sternum was fractured. She was in considerable pain for some time and this experience pushed her anger to the surface. When I visited her in hospital, she looked at me with a very angry face and asked me to explain how this 'loving God' could let this happen. I had no answers for her and simply stayed with her in her anger. Dee's anger was exacerbated knowing that the nun who was driving the car did not come away with so much as a scratch. Consequently, this 'proved' that the nun was a good person and Dee was not.

Dee had a short break from the sessions while she recovered from the accident. When she returned to therapy, she recognised more clearly how the 'drop-ins' were draining her. She also had some insights into the anger she carried and acknowledged the need to forgive some of the key people in her life.

So, all was going well … or so I thought. But you know the feeling that comes sometimes when you think that you can make ends meet – and then, somebody moves the ends?

Four days later, the ends were significantly moved to a place I had never visited. I quote from my notes from that day. Dee came to the centre, saying that she wanted to see me urgently. Luckily, I was available. She presented me with two drawings, including Image 2.

Image 2: Disgust/Thought Power

Dee told me that she was very angry with the person named on the drawing because she believed she had been spreading lies about her and Gloria, saying that they were having a love affair. Dee said she wanted to 'hurt' that person. She wanted to 'bend her spine' and that she could do it with 'thought power'. At the same time, she was also saying she didn't want to hurt her. She was actually on her way to visit the girl, who was an inpatient with back trouble. En route to the hospital, she came to see me.

Dee was not with me for very long when her mood changed. She said that she had been to a Pentecostal Church healing group. She declared that she was being plagued by demons and needed help to get rid of them. The minister told her, among other things, to stay away from people like Gloria. Dee said, 'I can't turn these poor people away, these people need help. I can't reject them the way I was rejected.' With that, she burst into tears. I encouraged her to stay with the feeling.

Dee held her hands up to her face as she cried. She began to talk to someone I couldn't hear. She said things like, 'I don't want to do that'; and 'I don't want to'. Her voice sounded like a little child, pleading and weak. I asked her who she was talking to. She didn't answer.

'Is it a man or a woman?' I asked.

'It's a man.'

'What is his name?' I prompted.

She replied, 'His name is Evil.'

'Can you tell him to go away and not to bother you?'

Dee said she wouldn't do that. She was crying again.

After some time I moved across the room and put my hand on her back. She was bent over, head on knees.

She said, 'He said that you were to take your hand off me.'

I said, 'I'll only listen to you. I won't take any notice of him.'

I felt her forehead, and she had a temperature, which I commented on. I sat down in front of her again and she said, 'Why did you say that Jesus was evil?'

I replied, 'I didn't say that. I would never say that.'

Dee's face had changed, she looked puzzled, and I could see that she either could not understand what I was saying, or she didn't believe me.

She said, 'Why are you trying to tear the heart of me?'

I said, 'I wouldn't do that to you, Dee, I love you.'

'No you don't. Nobody loves me.'

I asked, 'Do you love yourself?', to which she replied, 'I hate myself.'

I was sitting forward in my chair and Dee looked at me with disgust and moved as if to get away.

I asked, 'What's the matter Dee?'

Dee replied, 'I'm scared.'

'What are you scared of?'

'I'm scared of you. Don't come near me.'

I sat back in my chair and said, 'If that is what you want.'

Dee was looking at me now with loathing and hostility. She looked around the room as though looking at it for the first time. I thought that she was looking for something to break; she looked back at me with hatred. It seemed the fear had gone now. She began to shake a bit, as if convulsing. I left the room to call an ambulance.

When I returned, Dee shook, groaned and moaned. She slid gently off her chair to the floor. On her hands and knees, with her head in her hands, and she began to whisper, 'Jesus, Jesus.' She shook for a while. By the time the ambulance officers came, she was back in her chair again, looking very confused.

I asked, 'Are you back now?'

She didn't know what I was talking about. I told her that she had had a 'funny turn' and that I had called the ambulance just to check her out. She was still disoriented, but looked more like herself. Her face was softer and gentle, and she had lost the hard cruel look that had been present only minutes earlier.

The ambulance officers ran a few checks and reported that her blood pressure was 180/60. Her doctor was called and an appointment was made for the afternoon. The ambulance officer suggested she have her Dilantin levels checked. Apparently, this had happened previously, and Dee had been diagnosed as epileptic. I had seen grand mal seizures before – and, while this looked like a seizure initially, it did not follow the usual progression. After the ambulance men left, Dee said, 'I don't know why I'm going to the doctor, he won't find anything. They never do.'

She asked me what had happened and I said I didn't know. I told her some of the things I had seen; that she was frightened of me and thought that I was going to hurt her. She was shocked. She said, 'Did my face change?' I said that it had and she was very upset.

She said, 'It's back', but couldn't tell me what 'it' was.

After questioning Dee further, I realised that she had absolutely no memory of what had just occurred. I had seen her go through what looked like a personality change. I had been talking to someone who seemed like a total stranger, someone who did not know or trust me, and who could even have been out to hurt me.

I asked Dee if she remembered why she had come to see me. It took a few moments for her to recall. She was on her way to the hospital, she remembered, but she couldn't remember why. 'But why did I come to see you?'

I put the question back to her. Then she remembered the girl in hospital. The predominant feeling at the time was anger with the girl, and also fear of being rejected, just as she had been advised to reject Gloria.

So we talked about the rejection she felt by both her parents. She decided it was time to forgive them. She remembered the girl in hospital and decided that she should forgive her as well.

It took me some time to come to grips with what had happened. I hadn't seen anything like that before. I thought that it could be multiple personality disorder (MPD)*, but I wasn't sure. I was certain that whatever it was, it was triggered by Dee's intense feelings of anger and fear of rejection, which she expressed during the session. At the time I wrote:

'If it is a case of MPD then it would be appropriate to discover it, get to know it, make friends with it, find out how it benefits Dee and integrate that into the whole personality.

To buy into demon possession means that I'd have to turn into an exorcist and 'get rid of it' and therefore cut off any chance that we would have to integrate the benefits which it offers.'

It all seemed so simple and straight forward. But of course, it wasn't.

Looking back on this event makes me realise just how easy it would be to either run from this kind of experience – or worse still, launch into the role of exorcist and gear up to fight the 'demon' and expel it from the face of the earth. Sadly, I have to say that in my experience since then I have seen both options adopted, and always to the determent of the client, who most often comes out of the experience more damaged than they were before. As it was, Dee had already been influenced by the notion that she was being controlled by the 'evil one' and such strong beliefs do not go away easily or morph into something more comfortable to live with.

During the next visit three days later, before we sat down, Dee used a bottle of holy water to bless us both, saying we needed extra protection. She had a drawing which she labeled 'Confusion' and said it summed up how she was feeling. She was very concerned about her mental state and asked me at least four times if I thought she was crazy. I replied that I didn't think so. As we looked at and talked

---

*   'Multiple Personality Disorder' (MPD) was later to be renamed 'Dissociative Identity Disorder' (DID).

about the drawing, she seemed to experience a strong feeling, drifting off a little, and her expression changed. I gently called her name and she was able to refocus. She moved into this trance-like state at least five times during the session.

So we were entering a different phase of therapy. I didn't know where we were going and fortunately,

Image 3: Confusion

neither did Dee. At times we were both looking at a brick wall, unaware what was on the other side, if anything.

Two days later, Dee just dropped into the center. She had another drawing which frightened her.

She called it 'Beware'. It depicted a fish with spikes on the back and very sharp teeth. Inside the fish is a pointed dog's head and there is a smaller fish in the bottom of the big fish. She said that the big fish was another woman she knows and she is the smaller fish in the tail. She said that the other person was swallowing her up and controlling her.

Image 4: Beware

I thought that the 'other woman' was Gloria, or someone like her, so we talked about how she sometimes just needed to say 'no' when she felt drained by people like Gloria. The trance-like states continued and I continued to gently call her back. Looking back at this time, from my current vantage point, I think that she was ready to go onto platform 9¾ and explore the unknown parts of herself, but I wasn't. Maybe we both needed to feel safe before that could happen.

A week later Dee said that she was very stressed and that she almost didn't come. She said she felt like giving up. She brought three drawings anyway.

Image 5: Mistrust

Mistrust is a picture of herself and her blind grandmother and she said that while she was drawing it she remembered what her grandmother had said to her before she married Keith: 'If you are pregnant, I hope you die.'

This picture is the first that is directly related to a memory that she could recognize, and it provided a very important clue as to the nature of her childhood.

After we spoke about the drawings Dee told me that she had seen a very handsome man, who had grey hair and a wonderful smile. She said she didn't know if he was a friend or not. She looked like she was about to go into a trance but instead she started talking to someone else in the room. She said that it was the man she had described. I encouraged her to ask him who he was, but she said that he would not answer. Instead, she said that he had begun to argue with everything I said, and he told her not to take any notice of me. I felt I was facing some serious opposition and decided that the best I could do was to just keep asking her what was happening. At first she didn't want to tell me, but she did anyway. So, for a short time, the discussion was reduced to 'he said / I said / she said'. I have to admit it was very difficult to hold my nerve in this situation.

She seemed to be struggling with some very strong emotions. One foot was in perpetual motion as if she wanted to kick someone. I asked her if she still felt the rage we had talked about the previous week. She sharply told me that she didn't like being reminded of that, but yes, it was still there. The fading out occurred several times and I called her back each time, until she began to look at me with that angry, hostile face. She challenged me and said that she didn't trust me. Then she said, 'Why are your eyes like that?' She said they were green and that my face was distorted. After several episodes of fading out into a trance-like state, she threw her head back and said 'Dee is mad.'

I replied, 'I agree that you are in torment, but I could not say that you are mad.'

Image 6: To Pat, dear friend, sorry.

I was off work the next day as I had hurt my back and had to go to the chiropractor. Dee called into the centre and was told that I was sick. She came in the following day with a picture called *To Pat, dear friend, sorry.* She asked me if I had started to feel better in the afternoon and, of course, I had. The bone-crunching had worked. She was really upset because she blamed herself for my bad back. She said that sometimes when she is angry with someone, something happens to them. Then she said that she wanted to say something and she hoped I would understand.

She said, 'I really love you, Pat, but I am really afraid that I can't trust you. I just feel all this terrible rage inside me and I'm frightened.'

I said that she had every right to be angry because of all the terrible things that had happened to her. Learning how to express the anger without hurting herself or anyone else was the challenge. She gave me a hug and left.

Enter Lorna

I saw Dee again five days later and she had written a letter to me, which she read out. She said that she was very sorry about being so angry with me and for not trusting me. She also said that she had a good long talk with her other self and that her other self was called Lorna. She said that Lorna was the aggressive one. She had asked Lorna why she was so aggressive and Lorna said that she didn't like seeing Dee being pushed around and she only came out when Dee needed to be defended. I said that I could see how Lorna had been there for her benefit. As she talked about Lorna, I got the impression that she had made peace with Lorna and now they could be friends. I was also encouraged by the fact that Dee knew to open up a meaningful dialogue with Lorna – I took it as a very positive sign of some healing taking place.

She also said that she was beginning to understand why the members of her family were sometimes so frustrated with her. It seems that *Lorna* would make arrangements with them to go out and do something together – arrangements of which Dee had absolutely no memory – and when the time came, Dee became distressed and argued that she didn't make those arrangements at all. And, of course, she was right. She didn't, Lorna did. But how could the family know anything about her experience when Dee was only just beginning to realise it herself? Looking back, I can see that Dee had some degree of coconsciousness of her condition but there was a large part of which she had absolutely no knowledge at all. An excerpt from a letter she wrote to me expresses some of her confusion:

Dear Pat,

I have to put this down now before it passes from my mind. This afternoon I was sitting on the side of my bed when my daughter came in and asked me why I was crying. For a minute I didn't know what to say and then I said that I must have been crying in my sleep. She could see that I was crying and I didn't know. I don't even know why I was crying. How could I cry and not know I was doing it? I don't know what is going on, all I know is there is something, and I will soon know about it, how I wish I could work out how this body of mine works, but I guess that is something only God will ever know. Poor Pat, you sure got a doozy when you got me. I tell you these things Pat so that you may better understand, for my body is a mystery even to me. I want to know how my body works, this very different body, that can run away and hide if it so chooses, this is a little of me Pat, I feel you had to know these things for you are the one doing the work with God's help of course.

Dee told me how she first met Lorna. When she was a little girl, she was very lonely. She started to play with the little girl in the mirror and they played lots of games together. I could understand how this game developed until the time when Lorna was needed to stand up for Dee in threatening situations and how easy it would have been for Lorna to gain more strength as the years went on.

I also got the impression at this time that they had reached some kind of truce or agreement, and I felt that we were making significant progress. However, some truces are never meant to last; not for very long anyway. I knew we had a lot more work to do when she showed me the next picture.

three in one.

Image 7: Three in one

This picture looked like a big brick wall to me and I just didn't want to go there. I asked her what it meant and she said she didn't know. I referred to the title and she related it to the Trinity: Father Son and Spirit.

I was doubtful that it related to the Trinity. I had just been told about Lorna. Now, could I be seeing evidence of another one? A question in my mind at the time was how many more were there? I also remembered that in the case of Eve in the *Three Faces of Eve* (1957), the personalities always surfaced in groups of three, for example, the passive one, the aggressive one and finally, a synthesis of the two. Would it be the same for Dee? I didn't know; all I knew was that I just had to keep going until it all became a bit clearer.

Drawings

By this time I was also feeling overwhelmed by the sheer volume of drawings. The details were too much to deal with. Dee was confused, and so was I. The last drawing of the day was called *Confusion* and that summed it all for me.

Image 8: Confusion

However, I was soon to realise that drawing was an important part of Dee's healing. The very act of sitting down and allowing the drawings to emerge, was somehow loosening parts of herself that had never before been opened. Her discoveries were being validated and acknowledged, and while she experienced much anxiety and fear in the process, she also showed a lot of trust. The amount of trust she showed in me frightened me as well – I was afraid I would let her down and that I wouldn't be able to meet the challenges she presented. She may have said at one time that she didn't trust me. But she kept coming back. She kept drawing. I knew that if the drawings were an important part of her healing then I was to trust them also. So I had to put aside the drive to delve into them and analyse them as I had been taught to do, and just accept the gifts that they were offering to Dee. However, in retrospect, *Confusion* was really the first of the drawings that began to show the progress of our work together. I saw the overlapping oval shapes at the top as a positive sign. They spoke to me of the coming together of opposites, which I remembered from *The Healing Qualities of the Mandorla* which was part of a series of lectures given by the Jungian analyst Robert Johnson (circa 1980s, also in Johnson, 1991). In the meantime, another storm was brewing.

The truce between Dee and Lorna was soon to be sabotaged. In the very next session, Dee came in with six drawings which she almost threw at me. She was totally disgusted with the whole situation. She was angry with Lorna. It was Lorna who did the drawings, she said. Lorna was very good at drawing and Dee was hopeless. Lorna had the talent and she wanted it.

trying.   me.

Image 9: Trying

When we looked at the drawing *Trying* Dee became extremely angry and really hated it, saying it was such a 'horrible drawing'. In fact, I see it as the most integrated picture of the whole series. The number *Three* appears again in concentric circles, with the *Dove of Peace* in the centre, showering rays down on the little figure below with arms raised in praise and thanksgiving. Somehow, its simplicity felt right and full of hope, as well as the fact that Dee said that she had drawn it, meaning there had been no interference from Lorna.

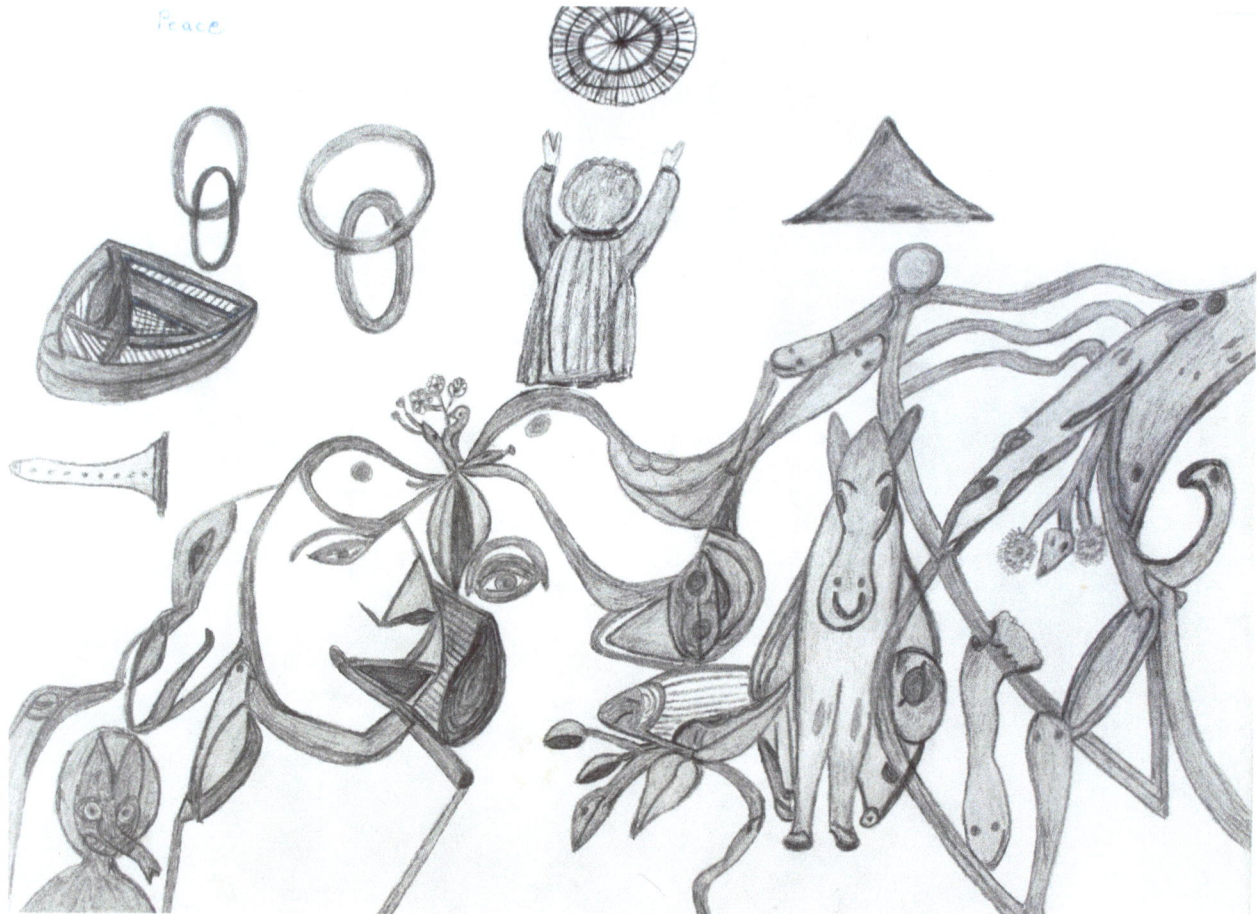

Image 10: Peace

The little figure with arms stretched up in an attitude of praise and thanksgiving had appeared in the series of drawings presented at the previous session, as well as some of the overlapping circles. So it is unclear who had drawn this picture. It didn't matter in the long run because they all came from the same source anyway. The main issue was that Dee was somehow 'feeling the differences' or maybe the 'separation' between herself and Lorna.

As we both sat and looked at all the pictures she had brought in, trying to understand them, I had the strong feeling that Dee was just as much in the dark as I was. So now, as I remember this, it is as though Lorna was standing on Platform 9¾, in that place of wonder and knowing, waiting for Dee and me to stop looking at the brick wall, take a good run-up and break through to where she was waiting for us.

A week later, Dee was angry with me. She was very anxious and it took a while before she could tell me what had happened. Gloria had been to see her. She claimed that I was talking to her and had told her things about Dee. So sabotage was coming from another source. It took most of the session to reassure her that talking about her with another person is something that I would never do, especially without her permission. Fortunately, she was able to accept my explanations and believe me.

The battle continued on several fronts.

memory of a painful time

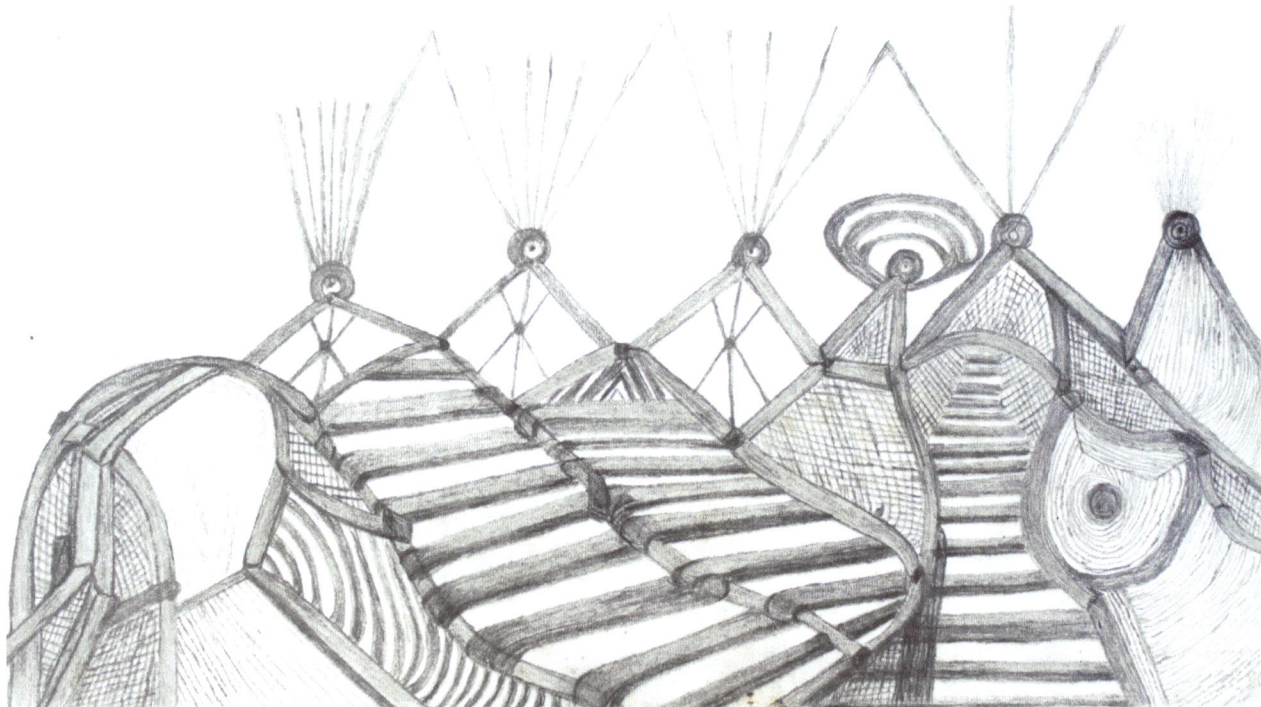

Image 11: Memory of a Painful Time

Memory of a Painful Time signified a change of pace in therapy. As we looked at this drawing, Dee remembered a time when she was seven years old. She nearly died from pneumonia and she said now that she wished that she had died. She began to shake and fade out, I called to her without response. She was crying into her hands and I could see that she had slipped into an old memory, so I went in with her. I found myself talking to a very lonely and sad seven year old. She was very sick and frightened, so I just sat with her and talked to her as I would with any seven years old. Dee's absence only lasted about three minutes. But at last, we were both on the same platform, sharing the experience. She was not alone in it – I was there with her, living the memory. Platform 9¾ can be a magical place and, like all magical places, it is very hard to stay there for any length of time, but we stayed there for as long as we needed to.

We had several trips onto Platform 9¾ after that. It was usually something in the drawings that would lead her to a memory. I found myself talking to children of different ages and with different concerns.

It was around this time I had a session with my supervisor who advised me not to get too fascinated with the so-called 'disorder'. She said that it was my job to find ways to integrate the different parts of the client. To become too fascinated with them, in terms of how they were formed in the first place and other details about them – things I didn't really need to know – could actually make things worse, not better. My supervisor impressed upon me that when I ask the questions out of curiosity, other alters can be formed, or existing ones can be extended, because of the feelings generated in the process – or worse still, in order to please me in some way.

So, while I was connecting with Dee at what seemed to be a deeper level, I had to learn to stay with her and not to sidetrack her by asking questions that would lead her into unnecessary details, in an attempt to try to piece together what I thought would be a coherent history. In just one session, we encountered three big issues: Guilt, Anger and Shame.

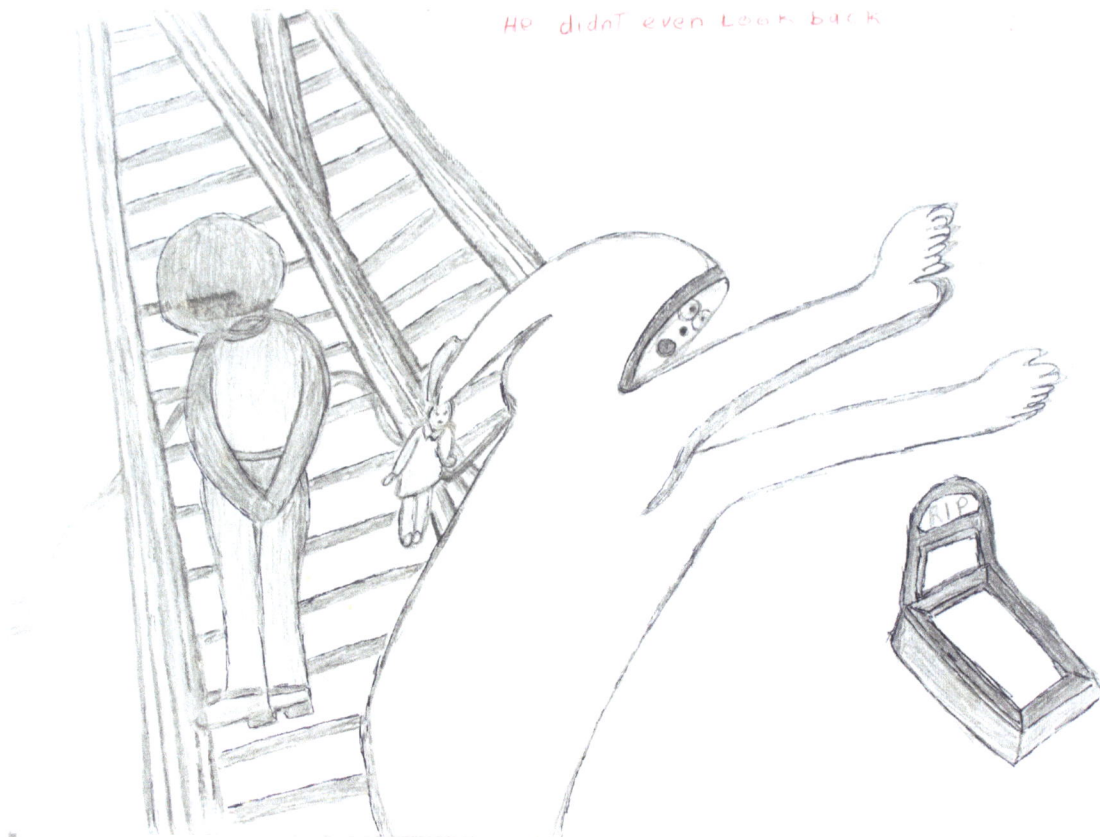

Image 12: He didn't even look back

Guilt

The picture entitled *He didn't even look back* recalls the time when Dee's husband Keith was in a lot of pain. Dee told him that it was alright for him to die and be out of the pain. He said, 'I'm so tired' – and then he died. The way she recounted the incident made it sound as if his dying happened immediately after she had told him that it was okay for him to be out of pain. She believed that if she hadn't said that to him, maybe he wouldn't have died. She blamed herself for his death, believing she had caused it. I learned that she carried a lot of guilt for things for which she was not responsible.

Big mouth

Image 13: Big Mouth

Anger

The central figure in the drawing has a big mouth. When I remarked on the length of the neck Dee said, 'It would have been after I wrung it.' Dee explained that this was the woman who tried to have an affair with Keith. As these memories flooded back, Dee stopped talking and just stared at me. The fade-out lasted about five minutes before her face began to soften and she realised she had been 'out of it' for a while. She had not said anything during this time and my sense told me to simply hold the space while she dealt with whatever she was facing, knowing that she would soon come back to our shared space. Being patient was not my forte, so I found it difficult not to intervene.

Naturally, the woman in the drawing was only one cause of the 'terrible rage' boiling inside Dee.

While she could easily recognise her as the object of such rage, it was difficult for her to name the figure as her mother, who Dee idealised and claimed as the best mother in the world. Dee hid her feelings and struggled to be honest about them. This realisation came slowly and not without great effort on her part.

Shame

As we looked at Image 14, *Goodbye Little Rabbit*, Dee told me she had done things that caused her great shame – things she just couldn't talk about, things she said I wouldn't believe if she did tell me. I repeated that I knew that there must have been many things that had happened to her; things that were not always her fault, but for which she carried the guilt anyway.

Image 14 : Goodbye Little Rabbit

After this, Dee reported that she was feeling very weak. She spoke about herself in the third person: 'Dee is getting very weak,' she said. 'It is as if she is fading away.' She said that she was seeing herself as the Little Rabbit and that she was disappearing.

Image 15 Run Little Rabbit, Run

The little rabbit appeared again the next week in the drawing titled, *Run Little Rabbit, Run*. The title of this drawing evoked strong feelings for Dee. A little rabbit appears in the top right hand corner with someone reaching out from behind a tree to catch it. I later learned that this was the subject of a recurring dream from her childhood, which she had spoken about early in our work together.

Image 15a: Run Little Rabbit, Run

As she explored this memory, I spoke to Dee at age twelve. She remembered how her uncle chased her through the bush till about 2am, before catching and raping her. He had instilled so much fear into her at the time that she was unable to tell anyone. She said she felt guilty because she 'got tired and had to stop running'. Her uncle was a soldier on leave, and she prayed he would get shot. He did get shot, so she felt responsible for that also.

For the most part we spoke about Rabbit in the third person. Sometimes she referred to Rabbit in the first person, and she expressed many strong feelings around the incident. When I felt clear that Dee had touched on and expressed as many of the feelings as she could, I changed tactics. The two dominant feelings were, guilt and being dirty, so I asked her to imagine *Little Rabbit* going down to the edge of a sparkling stream, clear as crystal. She watched as *Little Rabbit* got into the stream and swam across to the other side. At this point Dee started to giggle and I asked her why. She said that the Little Rabbit had turned into a white rabbit, and when she got out of the stream she was shining and bright.

Image 15b: Run Little Rabbit, Run

When Dee came out of the trance, she could see many more connections in the drawing. They were things we had talked about previously – only now I was hearing them from a different vantage point. She said the bottom section of the drawing (15b) was her mother's grave, and it reminded her of the mirror she used to talk to when she was little – the mirror where she first met Lorna. When her mother was taken to hospital, she was wearing a green nightdress and had a blanket over her. The blanket blew back and Dee thought, 'I hope she doesn't get a cold and die.' We again touched on Dee's belief that if she thinks something, it will happen. She realised that the little girl kneeling by the grave in the picture, is Lorna. Dee said that while she couldn't believe that her mother was dead, Lorna could.

I asked her about the five odd trees and she associated them with the five wounds of Christ. She then noticed the three distinct sections in the drawing: the tree at the top with the hand reaching for the rabbit; the five trees in the centre; and her mother's grave at the bottom. We talked about them and discussed the possibility that if her mother had lived then Dee may not have been raped. She could see why she had sought comfort in the church. Even though her understanding of all we had talked about that day had become clearer, she said she still felt torn – part of her could believe her mother was dead, but part couldn't. Dee left the session still giggling about the *little white shining rabbit*.

I was smiling too as it seemed that Dee was coming to the point where she could make sense of her drawings, especially this one. I thought that this drawing got right to the heart of the matter. It allowed us to explore the memory of being raped, and her feelings and beliefs about herself, which were connected to that experience. It pointed to the importance of Lorna's existence –it was clear to me that while Lorna was able to carry the truth of the mother's death, Dee could not.

The association of the five trees with the five wounds of Christ pointed to her attachment to the church, and also the confusion it produced in her. The church both comforted her in her relationship with Jesus and, at the same time, threatened to punish her for all the things for which she felt responsible.

The fact that she had begun to draw with coloured pencils was also significant, and did not escape my notice. Could it be that Dee's inner life was becoming much more colourful and a little less black and white?

Dee came in the following week saying that I must have done something to her, because she had noticed that her attitude was changing. She said she was feeling freer than she had ever felt before. She claimed part of this to be the result of resisting getting involved with her children's problems. She was growing in her ability to take responsibility for her own decisions and recognised that her children had to learn to do the same.

Dark Secrets.

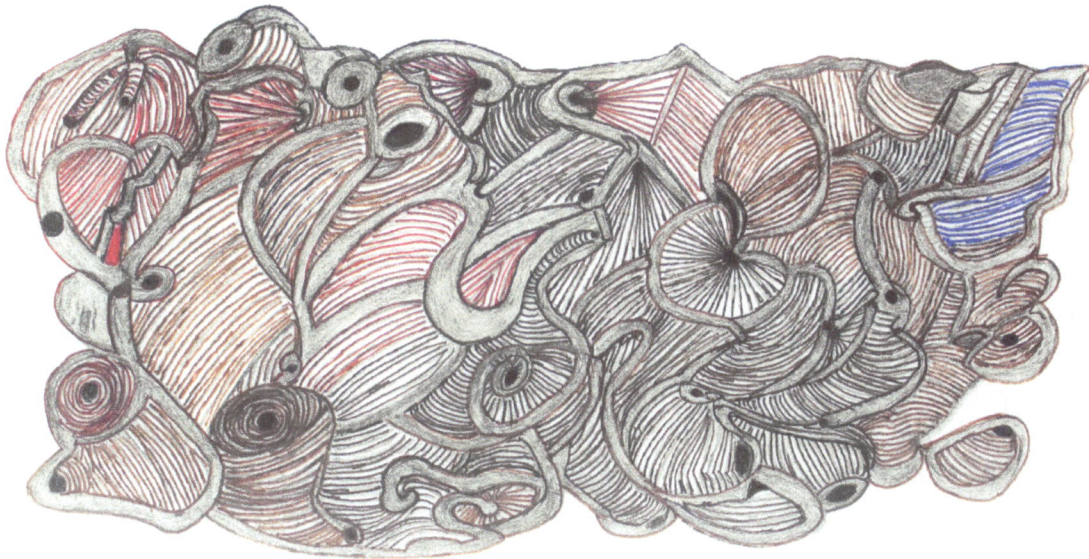

Image 16: Dark Secrets

More memories and strong feelings emerged once more around Keith's death, expressed in the next picture which she called *Dark Secrets*. Dee cried for most of the time she recounted the memories. She reverted to the belief that she only had to think of things happening, and they would come into being. She then inevitably blamed herself for causing the calamities. I challenged her on this and she said, 'Pat doesn't understand this.' At first I thought she was talking about me in the third person, which felt odd. Then I realised that maybe the 'Pat' she was talking about was another part of herself emerging. I was afraid that my interventions were causing more personalities to develop, and

I remembered the advice from my supervisor, asking myself if I was becoming too fascinated by the whole experience with Dee.

Again, Dee sobbed for a long time. When the sobbing was over, she looked at me in such a way that I knew she was unaware of what had just happened. I told her she had been crying about Keith. She said that while she doesn't understand all that is happening, one thing was clear – she knew that she and Lorna had to learn to work together and to stop all this competitive nonsense. She said that she needed Lorna's assertive nature, especially when dealing with her family. Could it be that I was at last seeing some healthy integration happening between Dee and Lorna?

Right at the end of the session I remarked on the picture and said how interesting it was that all the activity was happening in the bottom half of the picture.

Dee asked, 'What do you mean?'

I pointed out how the top half had nothing in it at all – it was a vacant space.

She replied, 'Pat, sometimes I really worry about you. Now I'm thinking that you are the one who is going crazy.' She added, 'The top half of that picture has lots of things in it.'

I didn't argue, thinking it was best to quit while I was ahead. After all, I was thinking of an interpretation of the drawing which could have taken us both into territory we didn't need to enter. The urge to interpret was very difficult for me to curb, but it was necessary to do so if I was to stay on the same platform as Dee.

In the weeks leading up to Christmas, the drawings, dreams and letters continued. The themes remained consistent. Dee's mourning for her mother and Keith, as well as her relationship with God and the church, set Dee on a roller coaster of emotions, and I could only ride along with her. At one time she said that it felt as if God and Satan were fighting over her, and that she was in the middle, being torn to bits. Some of the drawings brought a sense of calm while others didn't. Most of them, she just didn't understand at all.

During this time Dee named one of the drawings *If thy eye be single* – but she had no idea what the quotation meant or where it came from. It is part of a line from Scripture (Matthew 6:22): the full line is 'If thy eye be single thy whole body will be filled with light', and it is used by Johnson (1991) to describe the meaning of the Mandorla which is the almond shape formed by the overlapping of two circles. Each circle represents one of a pair of opposites, and the overlapping of the circles signifies the coming together of those opposites. I thought at the time that it could be another sign – or maybe an invitation – to integrate the different aspects of her personality. After all, could the 'eye' also be the 'I' or 'I am'? Whatever it was, I was very encouraged by this and even more so when Dee took the next step into the unknown.

She said that she had come to the conclusion that she had to let her mother go, and the idea of doing that frightened her because, for her, it meant that her mother didn't exist anymore. As we talked about the various images in the drawings and I called her by her name and she replied, 'Why are you calling me by that name?' I was taken aback. I apologised and asked her name, to which she replied, 'Mary.'

Mary's voice was different again. She seemed somehow softer and more contained. She spoke freely about Dee and Lorna, and seemed happy to do so. She said that Dee was weak and Lorna was sad. Of herself, she said that she was angry. I hesitated to ask why she was angry, mainly because she didn't seem angry – rather, she seemed to be contained and had a softness about her. I somehow felt safe with her and this reassured me that maybe the integrated Dee was beginning to show herself. I then spoke to Dee again, although at times I couldn't be sure to whom I was speaking. However, I took a risk, encouraging Dee to imagine that both Lorna and Mary had a gift for her and encouraging her to let herself accept the gifts they offered. I encouraged her to thank them and say goodbye. I also suggested to her that she would remember this meeting with the others, and also their gifts to her.

When Dee came out of the trance, she looked at me with the usual questioning look, saying, 'Three in one? That is not possible.' She said also that she felt pretty uncomfortable receiving gifts from people who are not there. We spoke about how we all have different facets that we show to others in different circumstances. I realised that I had become more directive than usual, and regretted doing so. I suppose my patience was being tested; I probably needed another supervision session to clear my head.

Dee came back to talking about her need – and fear – to let her mother go. So I encouraged her to write a letter to her mother.

The following week Dee said that she had attended a lecture on grief and bereavement and that many of her questions about her mother had been answered. She said that she still had a feeling of emptiness and strangeness on the inside, and she wasn't looking forward to the Christmas break, which would really test out her newfound attitudes to her family.

Dee's parting Christmas gift for me was the letter she wrote to her mother. It doesn't require much comment from me. Excerpts from the letter can speak for themselves, showing some of the struggle between Dee's need for her mother, her self-blame for what happened, her need to let her mother know of all the terrible things that had happened to her, her hate, and her desire for her to be hurt as Dee had been hurt.

My Dear Mumma,

Though it may take me some time, I feel God is now asking that I do write to you and I must go with my feelings. I loved you so very much my Mumma, and it hurt me so badly when you left. I don't know why God chose to take you but he has his reasons and I am not the one to question him. I did not think of that when I was a little girl, all I knew what that my Mumma was gone, I waited so long for you to come back, but the waiting became years and the child you tried so hard to make into a good solid person turned out to be a repugnant little monster. Do you know that my mumma, how I hated you for leaving me. You took my heart mumma do you know that? I was a little girl without a heart. I did not know what to do or where to go…

My life was shattered… I was caught in a trap…

You put me in Hell and Hell hurt, I am still in Hell…

I was pushed from one family to another… Not wanted, just another mouth to feed.

I was blamed for everything that went wrong…

No clothes to wear… a whole winter without a coat so I made myself hard so that I wouldn't feel the cold.

Being abused by my cousins… I am telling you these things because they are still eating away in my inside. I can't keep them locked away any longer. I said nothing of all these things, but I thought a lot, in fact, mumma, after you left, most of my life was made up of thoughts. My thoughts could not bring you back, but they could keep you alive. You came to me the night you died, didn't you. You stood by the bed but I was afraid and I didn't know it was you. You did not speak. What would you have said anyway? That you were sorry to leave me? Well that would not have been enough to make up for all that happened. If you hadn't left me all those terrible things would not have happened. I didn't realise how much I hated you until I was asked to write to you. I hope you could feel some of the hurt I felt because you did this to me, you, my kind and gentle mother changed my whole life and I did hate you for that. I am not even sure now if I can say I don't hate you and that I will, but just now I still hurt too much.

The list was long and heart-wrenching to read, and it must have been very difficult for Dee to write. Her idealised mother had disappeared and it didn't seem as if she could ever come to a peaceful solution. However, I did note that her anger with God had diminished somewhat and, at this stage, any shift in attitude was encouraging. But there was still some work to do with the drawings.

Stage 3: January to March

After the Christmas break I could see a big change in Dee. Not much had changed in the drawing department, however, in terms of volume anyway. Dee came in with nine drawings and I held my breath, bracing myself for the biggest session ever. However, something seemed different. Dee said that she understood the meanings in some of them but not in others and she wanted to tell me about the drawings before she 'got lost'. I could see that Dee was beginning to take some ownership and control of the process, and this was very encouraging. I have resisted the temptation to show all the nine drawings, choosing only a few of the most important ones. The titles of the others are sufficient to show the intention.

Image 17: Lord , fill the earth with your beauty

Dee felt uneasy about this drawing because it made her feel that she would want to kill a man. She said she saw this in the picture and wanted to change her attitude to the man she wanted to kill. She didn't say who he was, or what he had done to her.

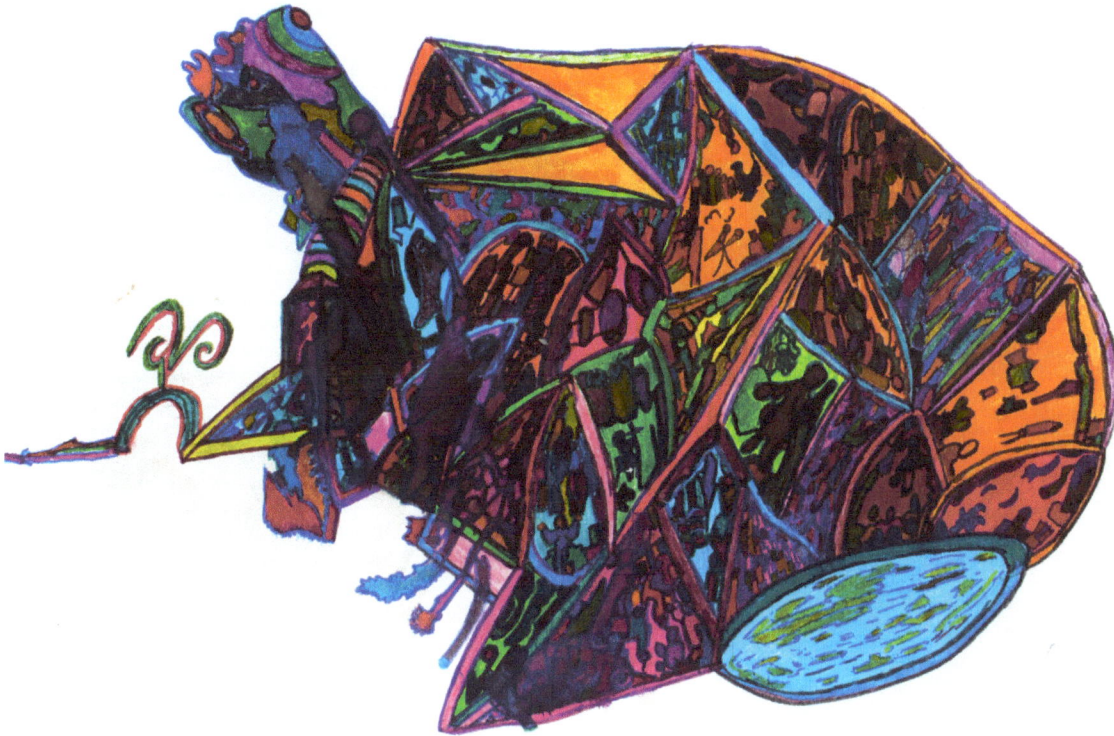

Image 18 : Lord, make me an instrument of your peace

In this drawing Dee said she saw the head of Satan and felt uncomfortable with it. She didn't want to talk about it, but thought that it was important.

Image 19: The wheel of justice brings a fountain of life

Dee drew this after she and her daughter had shared a spiritual experience. She didn't tell me about the experience, only about sharing it with her daughter. She said it was the beginning of her thinking that this year would be a very good one. She also said that she was feeling very hopeful that her life was changing.

Once I was weak but now I am strong

Image 20: Once I was weak and now I am strong

'At first this one worried me,' she said, 'but now I know what it means and it is good.' She said it gives her a feeling of being set free. The drawing showed her that she will not be in that cage anymore.

Image 21: I seek Thee Lord in so many places

Dee did not know what this one meant, except that it felt good that the face looks as though it is 'keeping its big mouth shut.' Whose mouth remained a mystery – I didn't ask.

Image 22: My Dream every angle has a meaning

Dee recounted a dream where she had many boxes and blocks to put together and she had trouble doing so. She said that she knew that some of the boxes had jewels in them, but she didn't open them. The red space at the centre bottom of the drawing is a furnace and it appears as though some of the jewels have been tipped out of it.

Image 22a: The Furnace and the Jewels tipped out

Dee said that a furnace is used to purify metals and refine gold, melting things down so they can be remolded, and that she sees herself as being involved in this kind of process. This dream and the picture are very important because they portray the alchemical process that takes place in psychotherapy. Carl Jung (2009) had much to say about the process that he observed in his clients and within himself. Unknown parts emerge and transform into something new and wonderful – that which is unknown becomes known, that which is unconscious becomes conscious. So we can see how once we were driven by the unknown or unacknowledged attitudes, and in this different place we can make better choices

Image 22b: The woman in the top left corner

The only thing that bothered Dee in the drawing was the woman in the top left corner, with a dark creature attached to her back. She said that the creature was not in the original drawing and she didn't know how it got there. She said that she thinks it means Satan is still on her back.

Image 23: Rainbow God's everlasting Covenant

Dee claimed this drawing as all her own doing and said it made her feel good. In other words, Lorna had nothing to do with it.

Image 24: Sing a new song to the Lord

Dee described the meaning of this picture as Jesus kicking her in the bottom and telling her to wake up to herself. In my opinion, she was really waking up to herself in the truest way possible.

Image 25: I thank you Lord for what you have done for me

The main feature of this drawing is the central building, which looks like a church without a cross. Dee said that there is light instead of a cross, and that the church is letting the light in. She felt good about that.

I was not surprised when Dee fell into a trance after we talked about the drawings. She got lost and I found myself talking to a person with a different voice again. She said she was Dee's 'True Self', so we spoke about Dee and what was happening to her, her fear of men, her loneliness, and so on.

True Self predicted that Dee would meet a man who she would become fond of, but that she would experience opposition from her family.

As we were talking, Dee shuddered. I asked her what was happening and she said she was down by the lake watching the gold speckles on the water. She had no memory of anything after the drawings, and I was in a dilemma as to whether to tell her about the conversation. I suspected that I shouldn't tell her, but I did anyway. Looking back, I think that I went alone onto Platform 9¾, leaving Dee stranded and afraid. The letter she handed me the next day confirmed that I had abandoned her and I realised with great embarrassment, that I had been manipulated in some way to sabotage the excellent work that Dee had been doing for herself. She was angry with me and also with God who, according to Dee, seemed to be telling her that she *had* to be in a relationship. What upset me the most was that I knew that the best healing for her was going to come from inside her, as the amnesia barriers between the alter-egos were breaking down of their own accord, not from the outside as a result of me telling her too much. Also, I had broken the rule of confidentiality between the personalities by telling her about the prediction made by the so-called 'True Self'. This prediction seemed to catapult her to a place where she didn't want to be. So far I have not read anything about the rule of confidentiality between the different aspects of the client's personality – I just think that the level of trust could be compromised if I report to one aspect what the others are saying: it can be experienced as a level of gossip and the cause of much damage. Trust is often difficult to earn and can so easily be lost when the 'gossip genie' comes out to play. Respect for all is then put to one side, treated as unimportant.

The next day Dee dropped in to warn me that Gloria was on the rampage against both her and me again. She cautioned me to be careful. I had to question, was Gloria the issue – or was Dee angry with me and fearful that her anger would cause things to happen to me? If the latter, Dee could have been stuck between wanting to punish me for bringing her the 'bad news' about a future relationship, while simultaneously needing me.

Two weeks after the so-called prediction of a relationship, Dee told me that she had met a man and had had several long chats with him. She was very ambivalent. At the same time she felt as though something was fading away from her. She didn't know what it was, but it made her feel a great sense of loss regardless.

The next day, she delivered another drawing and letter. She was very anxious. She said she couldn't give up her 'old habits' even though she knew they were wrong. Her rejection of the possibility of a relationship had shifted into a determination to do anything to make it happen. She wanted him, no matter what. So now we were facing apparent curses and deliberate acts to ensnare or physically damage others. While she perceived this kind of action as habitual, she also felt very guilty about it. I remembered all our conversations about the power of 'Thought Control', and the drawing she had given me many months before (Image 2). The struggle continued for several sessions. The trances continued and we spent several sessions on Platform 9¾ where I talked her through various experiences; some of which seemed to be long forgotten memories, some outside a time and a place from her past, and a couple which felt like a physical memory of her time in the womb. She came out of these particular experiences complaining of a terrible headache, as though she had been 'pushing against something'.

The following week Dee came in with another drawing which seemed to be quite significant. She said the drawing gave her a sense of having been protected and safe from the time she was born. I saw the Angel as a sign of safety, while I considered the rainbow as a promise of hope.

Image 26: Where have all the people gone?

Softly the leaves of sadness fall, gently I stoop and gather them all.

Stage 4: April to July

Almost twelve months after Dee's first visit, the change in her attitude and behaviour was significant. The drawings stopped. Dee said that her 'pencil had dried up.'

The idealisation of her mother crumbled, as demonstrated in Dee's letters to her: first, telling her how hurt she was, and then forgiving her for dying.

She added a few other people to the forgiveness list.

She recognised how the 'different persons inside' her were coming together, which may have been why she was remembering things from her childhood.

She also recognised that she had control over the voices in her head.

Dee's family relationships had improved and she felt good about that.

She had a deep sense of peace – something she had not experienced before.

She had found allies and foes in the drawings. She was able to accept the former and challenge the latter.

Some of Dee's experiences, she found difficult to talk about, such as feeling she was able to put her hand out and touch people who live in another different world. She said that there are many people in that place who she wouldn't want to touch, including her mother.

Another important experience for Dee was feeling a familiar rage – however, finally, she could allow the rage to be present without trying to block it out. As she persisted in allowing the rage, she saw herself standing in front of herself. The 'Dee' standing in front of her was very calm, and just looked at her. This gave her a jolt and she realised she could feel both rage and calm simultaneously – which I perceived as an interesting 'coming together of the opposites'.

There was still some confusion around God, but she still wanted to do only what God wanted her to do.

We began to revisit issues we had begun working on, with an occasional return to some of the previous distractions, such as when 'Creature' accompanied Dee to the session and made his presence felt.

Dee claimed to be beginning to accept Keith's death.

Dee said she no longer felt her grandmother controlled her; her curse was lifted.

Dee brought more drawings into the sessions, so I suggested she experiment drawing within the containment of a circle. She returned with her efforts (Image 27) and the vast difference was evident. This drawing could be called a 'mandala' which is of great significance because the circle is said to represent the Inner Self, the internal world of the drawer. It was used by Carl Jung (2009) for his own inner explorations. This mandala was the first of many that Dee presented in the final days of our association. I was struck by the colours, the structure, and especially by the title. This drawing showed me that there had been some significant change in how Dee was being reorganised from the inside out.

Image 27: There will be peace in the valley one day

July

Image 28: Strong and Constant is my love

Fifteen months after we had first met, Dee brought the following drawing which I had to study very closely before I could appreciate it fully. At first I thought it was another confusing conglomeration of meaningless shapes, until I noticed that the majority of the shapes were mandorlas – the almond-shaped space that appears when two circles overlap, as described by Robert Johnson (1993). Such a drawing depicts the thesis, the antithesis and the synthesis.

This drawing gave me a sense of the togetherness and integration that may have been occurring within Dee. The images are small and contained. There are many overlapping mandorlas in many different configurations. Looking closely, I could see a progression which I interpreted as a process Dee was going through as she was drawing it: trying to make sense of her experience of being both 'one' and 'many' at the same time. This is a difficult enough paradox to explain while looking from the outside, as I interacted with her – but almost impossible when trying to make sense of it from the inside world of her experience. Thankfully, the drawings captured the process quite well and the different shapes warranted a closer look.

Image 28a: Strong and Constant is my love

Here we see similar shapes, shown as separate and yet connected by smaller similar shapes. The progression appears to express a linear relationship between the alter-egos (aspects). However, from experience I know that there is nothing linear about the condition, and therefore this is not an accurate description of it. If only it were so simple!

Image 28b: Strong and Constant is my love

This is another way of connecting, repeated throughout the drawing, but it still doesn't seem to satisfy the need to portray the experience. The formation of the cross feels rigid, and it expresses a strong connection to Jesus. According to Dee's experience, this entailed not only a comforting presence, but also a suffering one.

rong   and   constant is my Lov

Image 28c: Strong and Constant is my love

This appears to be the most integrated image in the drawing and it is positioned at the top centre, under the word 'Constant', right next to another important image. Is this implying that there is now a 'constant and unified whole', that there are eight alter-egos, all equal in size and strength, held together by the one main and central personality? Each would have access to all the others, while being held together centrally.

According to my understanding of how drawings like this emerge, there is nothing 'accidental' about them (Furth 1988, Bach 1990). They come to us as messages straight from the unconscious, in an attempt to bring that which is unconscious into consciousness.

Image 28d: Strong and Constant is my love

I see this image as embodying hope and new growth. A healthy green plant grows out of a base of concentric circles. As mentioned above, this is top and central to the whole drawing and sits under the words 'my love'. Understanding drawings and applying a little interpretation can be helpful, but only if done retrospectively. It would not have been useful to Dee if I had told her all this at the time she showed me the drawing. I only mention it now to encourage my readers to learn how to think about drawings. Like dreams, they can: show progress; provide consolation; increase trust in the process; and give hope for the future.

Stage 5: August to September

Throughout August and September, Dee maintained her somewhat stable condition. She said she was 'feeling together'. There were no more drawings or letters during this time. She was planning to leave the region and move to the city with her daughter. The move was to be on a trial basis initially, to see if it worked for both of them.

I did not hear from Dee again until February the following year, when she called in just to say 'G'day'. I could see some big changes in her, as detailed in my notes.

She said that she feels a 'oneness,' a 'togetherness', that she has never felt before. She says that she is feeling very much at peace with herself. She is getting on with her daughter very well, in fact she is relating better to all her family. She says that she has cut herself off from the church, but that she is still very much in touch with Jesus. She says that she is listening more to what Jesus tells her, that she understands most of it and what she is hearing is not as frightening to her as it used to be.

Could these experiences be similar to the 'spiritual experiences' she spoke about when I first met her? I didn't need to ask her, her evident peaceful attitude as she told me about them was enough to communicate that there was nothing sinister or pathological about them. She also said that she was no longer losing chunks of time, and that the 'funny fits' haven't happened for a long time.

PART 1: TRAVELLING WITH DEE

In Summary

I learned much over this time with Dee.

I learned how to work with her using a simple method of validation and acknowledgement of her experience.

I learned not to worry too much about diagnosis or her various symptoms. In the end, it didn't really matter. Further, the diagnostic materials we now have at our disposal, were not available to me then. Dee's experience was real for her and so I had to learn how to enter into her reality. I challenged her a lot and tried to drag her into my reality, but it didn't really work. But somehow, she must have known that there was hope for me. Even though she was often angry with me, she kept coming back.

I also learned that an aspect/personality shift doesn't have to be as dramatic as the first time I saw it. Sometimes I was aware a subtle shift had taken place, only because a chance comment demonstrated that she had no memory of something discussed only minutes prior; subtle, but significant nonetheless.

I learned also that it is important to have respect for each aspect/personality as they presented, and to afford to each the confidentiality they deserved. At the same time I needed to remember that my conversation with one of them may be heard by one or all the others as well. It is always safe to assume that what I said to one, I was saying to all. So, it was important for me to not talk about the others, and to be respectful at all times. In order for me to successfully invite them into a collaborative relationship, they had to know I could be trusted.

As well as being trusted, I also had to learn how to trust the process occurring in Dee. I had to recognise that the barriers of amnesia were breaking down, and collaboration between the different aspects came about because of it. I didn't have to set myself the 'goal' of integrating them – indeed, I soon learned that any hint of 'integration' could be perceived by them as a threat of annihilation, and therefore should be avoided at all costs.

Most of all, I learned about the power in Dee's drawings. The drawings gave the hidden parts of herself a chance to express themselves. Now, after so many years, I could go back to each and place a deeper interpretation on them, but I consider that doing so would be both inappropriate and futile. I know a progression can be seen when we compare a drawing from the beginning of the journey to its conclusion. As evidenced below, my journey with Dee took us from *Torment* to *Come Take My Hand.*

Torment.

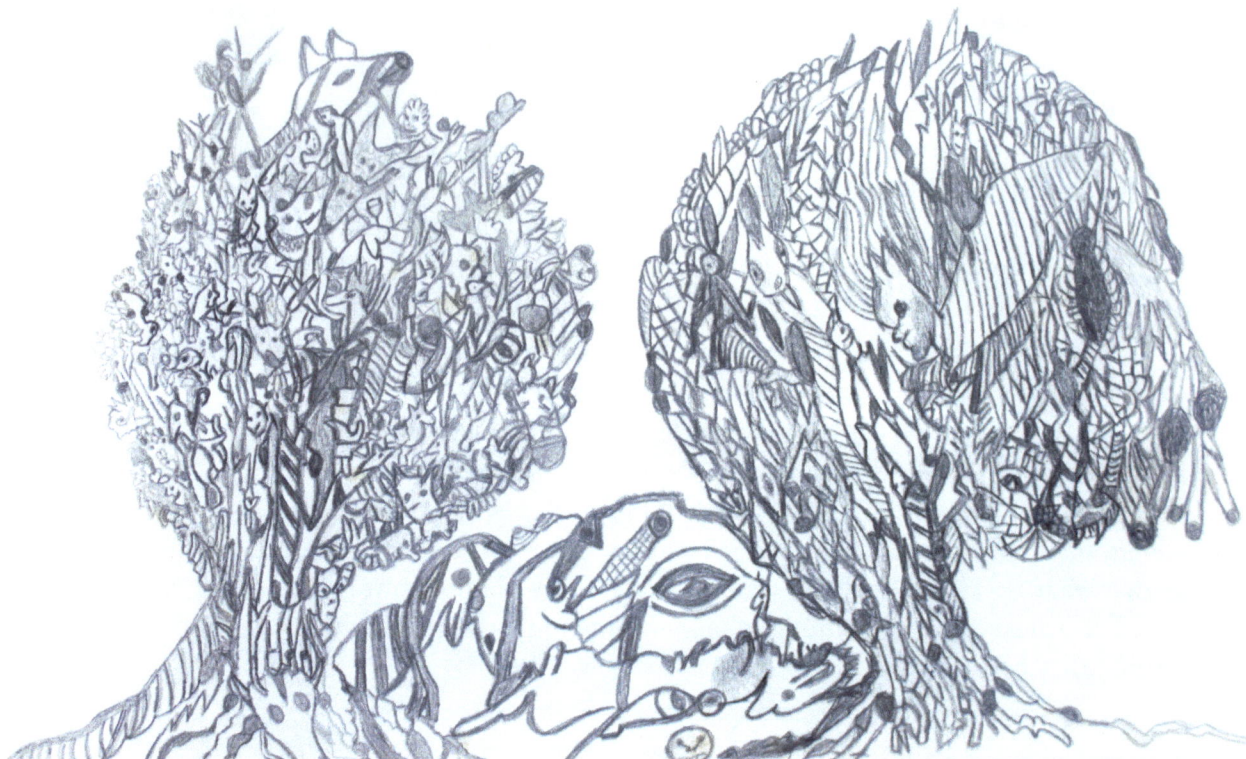

Image 29: Torment

Image 30: Come, take my hand

The whole experience confirmed for me something that I have known for a long time – if I want to take someone somewhere, I have to first meet them where they are. In this case we both had to be on Platform 9¾ before any changes could take place. There were times when we both felt as if we were facing the big brick wall. There were times when Dee disappeared through the wall and I could gently call her back. Then there was the first time when I found myself unable to call her back, so the only option was to follow … and that is when the magic and healing began.

63

As for me, walking through unfamiliar places is always a little scary. We walked through a few of those, but I am ever so grateful to Dee for the experience. I acknowledge her courage in facing the issues, and I am humbled by the level of trust she showed in me.

After so many years I can say, 'What a great journey we had together. Thank you Dee.'

Continuing the Journey

Dee's experiment living with her daughter turned out very well for both of them, and they decided to live together permanently. That was over thirty years ago and over that time I often thought of Dee and wondered if the work we had done together was still holding. Eventually, I decided to track her down, not knowing where she was, or even if she was still alive. I asked around the area, setting the bush telegraph in action, not knowing if it would be effective. It took about six months to kick in, eventually bouncing back to me with a phone call from Dee herself. She was delighted to think that I would even remember her, let alone wish to make contact. I promised to visit as soon as I was in the neighbourhood, and I made sure I would be, no matter how far I had to travel.

Dee was in an Aged Care facility, with family living close by. She was well and happy, and very settled in her new home. She hadn't lost her need to care for the 'lost' ones who were new to the place. She befriended them and helped them settle in. They seemed to know that they could depend on her to listen and understand what it is like to be lost and lonely, and missing familiar things. She said that she felt very sad when they died but delighted that they still came to see her. She said, 'I don't think they know that they are dead. So I just let them sit for a while and eventually they just leave.'

I hesitated at first to put any direct questions to her regarding the issues that brought her to my door, but in the course of the visit I learned that she hadn't had one of her 'funny fits' for 'a long time'. However, she said, 'There's just one thing I don't understand.' I was curious, so she explained, 'I don't understand why my grandmother could possibly think that it was alright to put a curse on me and my children.' I asked if it was truly lifted now – and yes, it was. Dee felt free of the belief that kept her trapped for so long – she was at peace with herself and with her God.

The last time I saw Dee she was very frail and it took her a little while to remember me, but her hug told me she remembered the most important things. We spoke about our time together and how strange it was for her to understand.

She said, 'I used to think that my mother was an elephant. Why would I think that?'

I replied, 'Well, mother elephants are very protective of their babies and you needed to have someone to protect you.'

She smiled when I reminded her of 'Creature' who used to come to the sessions with her – we both smiled. 'It's a good job that no one else could see him,' she laughed. 'The waiting room would have emptied out, quick smart.'

Dee was the first person I recognised as suffering from 'Dissociative Identity Disorder': many others may have slipped past me before Dee's dramatic entry into my life. Even now, I often miss the subtle changes in a client's demeanour or language that might alert me to the possibly underlying discourse. I'm not always looking for such things.

However, there have been many that have caught my attention and my work with them needs to be honoured in some small way. Most of the examples I share were not long-term clients. Some passed through my life only briefly. Our separate journeys crossed and, at the time, this seemed to be enough. I didn't have to hang onto them, and they only needed me for that short time. This reminds me of how I can get onto a train, connect with someone momentarily, and share deeply, until one of us leaves the train and we continue on our own separate journeys.

Yes, back to the Platform – and onto another adventure.

PART 2

Travelling with Jenny

I met Jenny during a workshop especially designed for people with a history of childhood abuse. It was a five-day, live-in experience and many topics were addressed. The main focus was connecting with the inner child who, for the most part, carried many secrets. Up to this point, there had been no way to share these secrets and indeed, in many cases, they were not even remembered. Humans have many ways to protect themselves and one very special way is to assign the most frightening experiences to a world beyond everyday experience. As we saw with Dee, her trauma was entrusted to Lorna, who became strong and at times very vocal in having her/their needs met.

So it was, too, with Jenny.

Because the week was so full, dealing with many heavy issues, we intentionally provided balance by giving the participants one day without any formal sessions. They were encouraged to do anything they wanted with the time. Toys and games were provided. Inviting the participants to play meant taking a risk, and calling the day 'play day' was also risky. Perpetrators of abuse often engage children in play which soon turns into a 'different' kind of game. Play time can be a very triggering for abuse survivors, often reminding them of something much more sinister.

So the toys were out and Jenny found a little tea set. She sat on the floor and quietly settled into making tea: carefully handling the little cups and saucers. She was totally engaged and other participants decided to join in. They were very attentive and caring. One of the participants alerted me to the fact that Jenny was so lost in the game that she seemed to be stuck and unable to get out of it to come to lunch. We sat with her until she could – we were late for lunch, but it didn't matter.

After lunch, Jenny came to me and asked for a chat. All the other participants had gone to their rooms for a rest: play-time can be exhausting. After a short team meeting, I found her sitting at one of the desks in the workroom. She looked very concerned, she had trouble talking, she would start a sentence and it would trail off to nothing. She would try again and once more she was unable to focus and for the words did not make sense.

Suddenly, Jenny leaned back in the chair. Her feet flew up onto the desk and she said, 'What a load of bullshit this is!'

I felt I had been hit with a cattle prod. 'Is it?' I asked.

'Yeah. Total fuckin' bullshit.'

'Hmm. Tell me more.' I was struggling.

'All that blah blah blah, bullshit. Drawing with the left hand stuff.'

'"Yes, I suppose that is a bit weird,' I said, trying to find a connection.

'Weird? Not just weird. Fuckin' weird. I'm just so fed up with all the fuckin' bullshit.'

'Yeah, it does go on and on a bit, doesn't it?'

After a long pause Jenny leaned forward, the feet came off the desk and she said, 'Hang on, I'm the voice inside her head, aren't I?'

'I don't know. What do you think?'

'Fuckin' hell. I think I am.'

Feeling relieved, I said, 'Well, I'm pleased to meet you, do you have a name?'

'A name? What would I be doin' with a name?'

'I don't know, I just thought you might have a name. You don't have to have one. I just thought you might.' After a short pause I said, 'So what is it like being inside Jenny's head?'

'Fuckin' hell. You have no idea.'

'You are right. I couldn't even imagine what it is like inside Jenny's head. So tell me.'

It didn't take me long to realise that I was talking to the aspect I have since named the 'street kid', the part of Jenny that got angry at the drop of a hat, lashing out and delivering a scathing attack on the person next to her, no matter who that happened to be. Jenny was known to have a volatile streak, and now I was getting to know the who lay beneath the behaviour.

The conversation continued for a while, so I asked her, 'Does Jenny know that you are there?'

'What! Of course she doesn't know. She is too stupid to work it out!'

'I think she is seeing a counsellor. Does she know that you are there?'

'That fuckin' stupid bitch wouldn't know anything. She is a total waste of space.'

'Ok. Well, I think that Jenny has to know that.'

'Fuckin' hell. Why would she have to know?'

'Well, you have been a big help to Jenny.'

'What!?' More colourful language. 'How the fuckin', hell could I be of help to her?'

'Okay. Let me guess. How often does Jenny get herself into very difficult situations? People taking advantage of her? Taking the piss? And you have to come in and get her out of it?'

'All the bloody time. She is just so stupid sometimes. It is unbelievable. I'm just so sick of it. But what can I do? I tell you, I'm just so fuckin' fed up.'

'I can understand that. So you could tell her?'

'What? Tell her? How the fuck can I tell her?'

'Well, you could write her a letter.'

'Fuck! Write her a letter? Are you mad? How could I write her a letter?'

'Well, I could help you with it. You have her book and pen on the desk in front of you.' She looked down at the desk and saw the book and pen. 'Fuckin' bloody mad if you ask me.'

She hesitated at first, so I began to feed her some words. She continued with it to the end. I didn't see her sign a name. When the letter was finished, I noticed her energy change, so I suggested we go out into the courtyard garden. We sat on the seat and our chat was brief. I directed her gaze to a tree in the courtyard with very colourful bark that changes colour when it is wet. She looked at it for a while and we felt the sun warm our faces. After a few minutes she said she wanted to lie down on the lawn. She stayed there for some time and went to sleep. I sat quietly, thanking the powers that be for allowing me to walk with her through that space.

The next day Jenny pulled me aside and asked if I could find some time that day to explain Multiple Personality Disorder/Dissociative Identity Disorder to her. I said I would be glad to do so. She also asked if her best friend could listen to what I had to say, so that she could remind her later in case she didn't remember some of it. I agreed and then put my mind to how I would actually do that. Yes, I had worked with Dee and had learned a lot in the process, but having to explain it to someone? This was the next challenge in my journey to understanding it more.

With the morning sessions over, some spare time presented itself. I sat with Jenny and her friend, who was also one of the team, both of them ready to hear a very simple explanation of a very complicated subject.

I drew a circle, and explained this is often used to represent the whole self, or the entire psyche, incorporating every aspect of the person. I divided the circle into segments, like a pie chart and then gave each piece of the pie a title, which could be a state of mind or an age. I explained that we all have different personas for different circumstances. For example, if I am talking to someone in authority, I speak with respect; with my friends I might tell a joke or complain about my arthritis; the bank manager will see a person who knows what she wants to do with the money she wants to borrow and how she will pay it back, and so on. In the pie chart for MPD/DID, there could be all of those listed above, but it may also contain aspects which could be called mother; ten year old child; child in the cupboard; sexy teenager; angry person; or playful child. Not all the different segments actually know that the others are there – the lines dividing them depict amnesia barriers. So if one of the aspects has an experience, the others may not know, and thus, confusion reigns and often be the cause of arguments with others: such as members of the family, who do remember what the person with DID has forgotten.

I tried to keep the information brief and clear. Jenny took the diagram and we returned to the business of the program. I wondered how she would respond if and when she found the letter from her 'protector/street kid'.

The next day when everyone was leaving to go home, Jenny pulled me aside and said, 'I have a message for you.' I was curious. She said, 'Angela told me to tell you that you are very good at keeping secrets.' I think the smile on my face told her all she needed to know. The 'protector/street kid' had a name – Angela.

Given the present situation: me running an experiential program and Jenny as one of the participants, the intervention was appropriate and sufficient. My personal rule was not to become too fascinated with the condition; I did not need to know how Angela came to be, or in what other circumstances she comes out and takes over. It was essential that Jenny know that Angela was there: opening her up to the information was the important thing. It was important for Angela to connect with Jenny on her own terms and in such a way that Jenny could take it in and process the information on her terms.

It could be said that I left a lot to chance in giving her the information as I did. At the same time, I simply had to trust the process: Angela chose to come out and, in a way, attack me. My response to that exposure was vital for facilitating the process. I was able to recover from the shock quickly; remain attentive to what was happening; recognise the gem that had just been handed to me; connect with Angela and let her know how important she was to Jenny's survival; and take the opportunity to make it possible for Angela to communicate with Jenny in a simple and powerful way.

Without laboring the point too much: the alternative was not an option for me. Jenny asked me for information about MPD/DID: the information I gave was very simply illustrated. I could have extended that session by giving Jenny a diagnosis and by suggesting that she tell her counsellor at the very next visit. I could have told her about the conversation I had with Angela, just to be 'professional', in effect taking the emerging self-agency away from both Jenny and Angela.

To my way of thinking, all of this would have been totally counterproductive. The most effective way to deal with this incredible survival strategy is to facilitate the process for inner aspects to reveal themselves if and when they choose to do so. The healing has to come from the inside, it would have been destructive to 'spill the beans' on Angela. I did so like Angela for her no-nonsense approach to getting things done, and I often think of her fondly.

Many years later Jenny's friend, who had sat in on the interview, told me of an example of Angela's 'no-nonsense' approach to a situation. They had been driving and Jenny wanted to stop and have a cigarette. She hated the habit and had tried to give it up. Frustrated, the angry familiar voice shouted, 'Which one of you fuckin' bastards is the smoker? I'm sick of putting up with it. So fuck off and stop it.' What an ingenious way to quit, don't you think?!

Jenny never needed to light up after that little intervention. Well done, Angela!

PS I have since learned that the self-agency that Angela instigated was carried through to her counsellor who, according to Jenny the last time I spoke to her, was a great support for her at that time.

PART 3

Travelling with Joe

Joe was in his early fifties when I met him. He had been to several workshops to help him deal with the issues that arose from his early childhood and teenage years. He was tall, strong and capable when it came to fixing things around the centre, confident in how he presented himself, and considerate of his fellow participants. He soon expressed the desire to attend training to be a support person on these workshops. At the end of the training week, Joe asked if we could chat about something I had said that he didn't quite understand. We found a quiet place and the point of clarification turned into something else.

Joe began to relate an experience he had had when he was about fifteen. He had earlier disclosed that his mother was his main abuser while he was growing up. He couldn't do anything right and nothing would please her. The incident he spoke about occurred one afternoon when he arrived home late from hockey practice. His mother flew into a rage and attacked him with the hockey stick. Joe's memory was strong and quickly turned into a flashback: he was experiencing the incident in the present in a very real way. He went down onto the floor. I followed, trying to soothe his pain as he relived his mother thrashing him. It took some time for him to return from that experience.

Later, he told me that he had dissociated: part of him was standing at the door watching us on the floor, and the only thing that brought him back, was feeling my tears on his back.

Recognising the ability to dissociate opened more avenues for him to tackle in a therapeutic setting, and he started working with me privately.

Joe always arrived with an issue he wanted to explore and his 'protocol' to enter into it was always the same. He sat upright, with a straight back, head bowed just a little and hands held in front of him. He addressed me in an old-fashioned, formal kind of way. The image of a monk always came to me when he sat and spoke this way; I felt I was in the presence of the Wise Old Man archetype.

'Good morning madam. I am honoured to be in your presence this day.'

'I too am honoured to be here, Sir," I would reply. And so the conversation continued. He often spoke about Joe in the third person and together we worked out some strategies to help him with his issues.

Mostly we spent the time uninterrupted, except for one day when he stopped and said, 'Pardon me, madam, I am finding it very difficult to concentrate.'

'What is happening to distract you sir?' I asked.

'There is a baby crying and I am disturbed by it.'

'A baby crying?' I asked. He nodded and I said, 'Can you wait while I attend to it?' He nodded. So I started to sing a lullaby.

How can anyone ever tell you, you are anything less than beautiful?.

When I finished singing, we continued the conversation uninterrupted. At the end, when he was preparing to leave, I asked about the baby.

He smiled and said, 'She is asleep.'

I understood from this interaction that Joe's abuse had started very early in his life, in the cradle I suspect. For me, there is nothing more heart-wrenching than the cry of a baby left to soothe itself, when nurturing and probably feeding is necessary, but the cold, unattached parent is unavailable. I came to understand that neglect can be the most devastating form of all abuse.

The incident also confirmed for me that all aspects of a person could be paying attention to what I am doing and saying, so I need to be very careful what I say and how I say it. With this belief comes respect, so I need to pay attention to whom I am speaking. This is not always possible, as shifts can be very subtle and unrecognisable as distinct from each other.

Joe has a very strong need to investigate every aspect of his condition, to the point of exhaustion. One of the things I have noticed with some people with ready access to their 'others', is that they are desperate to know how many aspects they have. I think this is a natural phenomenon and sometimes I wonder whether knowing this might actually make things worse than they are already. My reasoning behind this is that in the fascination of getting to understand dissociation, we can lose sight of how it develops in the first place. For example, when a child is being used and abused for the malicious delight of another, he or she will feel overwhelmed and terrified: causing a split, an escape to a safe place. Hence, it must follow that if the person is put under any undue stress during the process of investigation, further 'splits' may occur. I remember a conversation with one such person, who was not a client of mine but was in therapy. He said, 'I have 100 different personalities.' Now I am not denying this fact, but what I saw appeared to be a form of boasting about the quantity – as though he were winning some kind of competition.

This was a concern I had about Joe, at least to begin with. I soon lost the fear or judgment when I realised how he went about discovering his 'others'. At the time, Joe lived in a house that had access to a stream at the bottom of his patch of land and he would make daily visits to this place, early in the morning, to sit and meditate. It was a great way of setting up his day before going to work.

Joe used the same process to set up our sessions – hence the appearance of the Monk or the Wise

Old Man I described earlier. Being settled in his place, he would begin by making it known that he wanted to meet the children who helped him to survive his childhood. He would always begin by thanking them for what they did for him, and he would encourage them to come and meet him. And come they did. They came one by one, except for the twins; they were hiding behind the bushes; locked away in a small dark cupboard and always shy. When the children couldn't speak to Joe, they spoke to me so I also ended up in the dark cupboard showing this terrified little boy how to use the pencil torch I gave him, to help him see in the dark.

This process was not a competition: Joe was inviting and caring and learning about his parts; welcoming them; holding them; vowing safety for them and promising to teach them how to play. They even have a house to live in with a house-mother; the she-wolf who stands guards against intruders, and a very safe mother bear with two cubs for playing.

Joe has written about this in much more detail, in a form that I hope will come to light soon. In reading his manuscript, I came to understand more fully the process he engaged in in his investigations. Joe's daily meditations are key to the process: putting himself in the same place to connect with his inner voice/guide, he would ask the questions and the guide would answer. Sometimes the voice would simply interrupt him and inform him what needed to be written. This process is very similar to what Carl Jung called 'Active Imagination', which can be very powerful, especially when working with dreams. It is a process that led Jung to investigate his own way of being in this world, leaving behind a template that we can follow now, many years after his death.

The bottom line is that a determined investigation for other aspects can be done wisely and respectfully, with the understanding that different aspects can be encouraged to make themselves known to the 'Big Person on the Outside', as Joe's aspects called him.

PART 4

Travelling Reflections

Looking Forward

I can only hope that my written offering can bring into focus a few things about dissociation that are sometimes either not recognised or are completely overlooked..

Dissociation, even in its most severe form, is a normal reaction to a very abnormal situation and is always the result of severe trauma, usually experienced in childhood. That does not mean that everyone who suffers abuse becomes dissociative and develops other discrete aspects of their personality, but it does lay down the foundation that helps the victims survive. I consider that dissociation is the most wonderful and incredible survival technique that our mind/body/psyche can provide. Yes, even having seen extreme examples, I still hold that it is a normal reaction to an abnormal situation.

Dissociation is normal in the sense that everyone does it. It could also be called daydreaming. Anyone who has bought a ticket in the lottery does it. Ask anyone what they would do if they won the millions on offer, and the list is long; pay off the mortgage; throw in the day-job; buy a house for the kids; have the best holiday ever; find a cure for cancer; donate to their favourite charity, or just cash it in, stuff it under the mattress and keep it for a rainy day. This is daydreaming – a benign form of dissociation.

Then there is another form of dissociation, which is sometimes called 'Highway Hypnosis'. I have experienced this on many occasions, and it can be very scary. Picture the scene. I had three children in school and two in preschool; my father-in-law was dying in a nursing home close to where I lived; my husband was critically ill in a hospital 45 minutes' drive away and the business I had to attend to was halfway between the two locations. Every day for about six weeks I had to organise the kids; visit the father-in-law; check in on the business and make my way to visit my husband and update him on everything. So what was the scary bit? I always travelled the same route to achieve these things, yet there were many times when I suddenly realised that I did not know where I was. I didn't know if I was on my way to the hospital to see my husband, or on my way home to pick up the kids and somehow get some food on the table. I quite literally did not know whether I was coming or going. I quickly learned not to panic at this stage. Something told me to just keep going, be steady – just keep going. It felt like there was a voice in my head that said, 'It's OK. Very soon you will see something that you will recognise and you will know then where you are.' And so, I did see something and the crisis was averted. The cause is easy to establish – stress and exhaustion go to the top of the list. Thinking about this now, I can thank the voice in my head (auditory hallucination?) and also the power of procedural memory. Having travelled the same route for so long, I felt like the car actually knew its way and having me at the wheel was almost incidental.

So, to the person reading this book. If you are experiencing times when you realise that the day has gone and you can't remember what you were doing; if you find clothes in your cupboard that you don't remember buying; if you meet people who are convinced that they know you and have known you for a long time and you can't remember them; or if you are having stressful conversations with members of your family who are convinced that you did do, say or agree to things that you really can't remember, then please seek help. You may have some trouble finding the right person to help you, but believe me – more and more therapists are familiar with the situation you are experiencing.

If you are a therapist and what I have written here is ringing bells for you in terms of some of your clients, then don't forget to organise some supervision, not only so you can gain more in-depth information on dissociation, but so you can also have a time where you can debrief on what you are feeling as you walk alongside your clients. In my early days with Dee, I spoke to a psychiatrist and he said, 'No. That is impossible. It is too rare.' Later I spoke to a Jungian analyst and she gave me the advice I needed at the time. She said, 'Don't get too fascinated with the condition. If you ask too many questions you could put her under stress and that could cause further splitting.' Just recently I sought supervision with another psychiatrist and he said the best thing ever: 'I work with whoever is in the room.' That says it all to me. Even if they 'split' in front of you and you notice that, stay with the person who is doing the talking. Attend to that person; be with him or her, as that is where the healing is.

Remember that for anyone, therapist or otherwise: there is power in the creative process, and it doesn't matter which form it takes. Drawing, writing or playing with clay can give the unconscious material permission to come to the surface. Music, played or listened to not only presents imagery of things unknown to us, but can also assist in the expression of thoughts and feelings associated with the imagery. Processing this information can help us take a good look at our lives, make better choices, and open new avenues for creativity and expression.

I would like to point out that the biggest danger for someone like Dee is to have a diagnosis dumped onto to them by someone who would consider the contacts she had with the people who had died to be psychotic disturbances: heavy medication would follow, along with the side-effects, and then more medications to counteract those. I can't consider Dee's experiences with spirits to be pathological: for her it was normal. The fact that I can't see them doesn't mean they don't exist. After all, I grew up in a world where saints and martyrs experienced life in an extraordinary way; they saw visions; witnessed miracles and performed them; suffered unbelievable torture and died bravely without denying their faith in God. Being able to meet Dee right in her experience was more important than hammering out the 'truth' according to the rest of society in the general medical and mental health system in particular. Dee could have been diagnosed as 'delusional' or 'psychotic' and told that the experiences were 'all in her head', and the end result would have been to deny the healing and integration that she eventually was able to reach for herself.

At this point I can't resist quoting from the last of the Harry Potter books and movies. Harry has sacrificed his life to prevent any more deaths at the hands of Lord Voldemort, and he finds himself on King's Cross Station where he meets the also-dead Professor Dumbledore. The professor tells Harry he must go back and finish the job he had started.

'Tell me one last thing,' says Harry. 'Is this real? Or has this been happening inside my head?'

Dumbledore beams at him, and his voice sounds loud and strong in Harry's ears even though the bright mist is descending again, obscuring his figure.

'Of course it is happening inside your head, Harry, but why on earth should that mean that it is not real?' (Rowling, 2007)

When I saw this on the big screen, I almost stood up and cheered. I wish I had.

Dee's Last Word

IMG 1570 Brown Eyes with a rainbow smile. Guess who?

Dee willingly gave me permission to tell her story and because she had taught me so much, I think it is fitting to give her the last word. We were a long way into our journey together when she took the chance and presented me with this drawing. I somehow knew that I would not escape her pencils, though by then she was using paints as well.

Dee used to call me 'Brown Eyes', and she got that right in the drawing, however, I have to declare that I never wear earrings. I do like the Mandorla shape, though, and all I have to say now is: 'Picasso, eat your heart out. You never had the chance to paint me. Dee did. And I am delighted with the result.'

Thank you, Dee, for the rainbow smile, it will never fade while you are in my memory.

Bibliography

Bach, S., *Life Paints Its Own Span: On the Significance of Spontaneous Pictures by Severely Ill Children,* Zurich, Daimon Verlag, 1990.

Furth, GM, *The Secret World of Drawings: Healing through Art,* Boston, Sigo Press, 1988.

Johnson, Nunnally (Director), *The Three Faces of Eve* (movie). Cast; Joanne Woodward, Lee J. Cobb, David Wayne, Adaptation of a case study by Corbett Thigpen and Hervey Cleckley, Released; 1957.

Johnson, RA, *Owning Your Own Shadow: Understanding the Dark Side of the Psyche,* New York, Harper Collins, 1993.

Rowling, JK, Harry Potter and *the Philosopher's Stone,* London, Bloomsbury Publishing Inc., 1997

——, *Harry Potter and the Deathly Hallows,* London, Bloomsbury Publishing Inc., 2007.

Thigpen, CH and Cleckley, H, *The Three Faces of Eve*, New York, McGraw Hill, 1957 in Altrocchi, J, *Abnormal Behavior,* New York, Harcourt Brace Jovanovich, Inc., 1980.

www.ingramcontent.com/pod-product-compliance
Lightning Source LLC
Chambersburg PA
CBHW060820270326
41930CB00003B/97